We are the Dreamers

The Double Curve design is an element unique to Mi'kmaw art. Frank Speck describes it as a "horizontal bar in the centre of the enclosed area supported on two out-curves from the bottom. This interior pedestal, as it were, seems to form a mark of identity for the Mi'kmaw designs, though we are, as yet, at a loss to explain it."

RITA JOE

We are the Dreamers

RECENT AND EARLY POETRY

BRETON BOOKS

Editor: Ronald Caplan
Production Assistance: Bonnie Thompson and Tyana Caplan-Panthier
Linguistic Consultant: Dr. Bernie Francis
Typesetting: Glenda Watt

The back cover photograph was taken at the Chapel Island Misson, during the procession carrying St. Ann with Mi'maq flags flying—courtesy *Cape Breton's Magazine*, Issue 40. The Double Curve images come from petroglyphs (rock drawings) in Ruth Whitehead's lovely book *Micmac Quillwork* (Nova Scotia Museum and Nimbus Publishing). Poem 18 on page 75 is a reworking of an account of the Mi'kmaw by Nicholas Denys, first published in 1672.

Le Conseil des Arts du Canada DEPUIS 1957 | The Canada Council for the Arts SINCE 1957

We acknowledge the support of the Canada Council
for the Arts for our publishing program.
We also acknowledge support from Cultural Affairs,
Nova Scotia Department of Tourism and Culture.

Canadian Cataloguing in Publication Data

Joe, Rita, 1932-
We are the dreamers
ISBN 1-895415-46-2
1. Micmac Indians — Poetry. I. Title.
PS8569.0265W4 1999   C811'.54   C99-950235-2
PR9199.3.J55W4 1999

BOOK ONE

We are the
Dreamers

continues next page...

v

BOOK TWO

Poems of Rita Joe
POEMS TO 1978

BOOK ONE

We are the Dreamers

I am the Indian
And the burden
Lies yet with me.

The invisible line of the burden is the central idea which keeps banging against my head and cannot drop unless I am satisfied. The satisfaction does not seem to materialize with each problem I try to conquer. The minor self-war has turned into a mountain, I cannot reach the top. The top being my own satisfied conclusion.

That I think is what keeps me going, the day to day problem solving, even looking for it. Like tearing my own poetry apart, meandering into different directions, pecking there or just look-ing, the many trails too many to take on. But when another day comes there is that spirit rising again to take on any cause just to see if it can be slowed, dumped or won over. The tired body now broken, the spirit hanging on just so it can be pushed to the limit, if not for me but others, the endless trail into another century, then maybe, just maybe....

Uncle Antlo'

I received word from Conne River, Newfoundland
To record a Micmac hymn for a burial
An old man in his eighties wanted to hear.
He remembered the hymn in his early years,
Now that he was old, he longed to hear again.
So I took a tape recorder to my neighbour next door,
I knew he sang the hymn once in a while.
His wife Mary said that Andrew was working outside.
I saw a circle of land cleared away, a work horse there
My people used it for shaving, a handmade te'sipowji'j
Andrew was using a drawknife shaping an axe handle.
"Uncle," I said, "Would you sing a song for me?"
He put the drawknife down and a kitten jumped on his lap.
I recorded him and stood back admiring the view,
The old man with the small kitten, brilliant sunshine.
To me the view was spiritual, so simple but happy.
In my mind I saw heaven, the deed so kind.
My old friend said yes readily, to someone he never knew.
The Micmac people are always like that, so ready to share.
For an instant my culture I held dear, will always hold.
I want to share this story with you
Because in the future for my people, I wish you care.

te'sipowji'j — a handmade work horse with
hand levers, a vise at arm's length

2

Ntus   Theresa Ann

In October 1992 while I was in Tobique N.B.
I had a conversation with a man who had a hard time.
He became my friend, telling me his problems.
I felt pity, we were in the same situation
The hardship brought on by drugs and alcohol.
Sometime later we were doing a sweat,
I knew my friend was one of them, wishing him luck.
At the third formation I felt a small baby get on my lap
Instantly I knew it was Theresa Ann
My baby who had died recently.
"Thank you for coming," I said. "I am doing okay now."
"There is a man here who needs help," I said
"Give him a tiny piece of your heart."
At that instant I felt her leave my lap.
At the same time I heard weeping from the other side.
Later when we were finished I wanted to be alone
To experience the spiritual feeling I had.
My friend told me that while he was in the sweatlodge
A small baby came to touch him on the arm.
A beautiful feeling spread throughout his body.
I thanked him for telling me, I knew it was Theresa Ann
My beautiful baby who helps us each time we ask.
My ntus who suffered for thirteen months, then left
To go to the spiritual place we all want to go.
My baby Theresa Ann, the little native angel
With my Niskam, the Kji-saqmaw of all that is good.

ntus — my daughter
Niskam — God   Kji-saqmaw — Grand Chief

3

She spoke of paradise...

She spoke of paradise
An angel friend.
She spoke of Kisu'lkw
And weji-uli-Niskam
The names I always knew in mind
Completing the picture
But of man's true brotherhood
Her practice was not mine
Today I teach
To love is to sit with me

Kisu'lkw — Creator
weji-uli-Niskam — Holy Spirit

A True Story

A Mi'kmaw boy of eleven years
Stood in the woods of Eskasoni
A cold sleet of rain had fallen
During the night in the woodlands.
He was cold and shivering
Cold and shivering in the woodlands.
He looked around unable to find
The maple tree in the woodlands.
A clean maple to strip for baskets
A clean maple in the woodlands.
He bowed his head and said a prayer
A sad prayer in the woodlands.
I cannot go home without the maple
Without the maple in the woodlands.
"Kisu'lkw I know you are there
I know you're there in the woodlands."
And there before him stood the maple
Ta'n mu etenukup in the woodlands.
He cut the maple without the cold
Without feeling in the woodlands.
His parents were glad there will be baskets
Baskets to sell.
And from hunger they will survive
Because of the woodlands.

Ta'n mu etenukup — where it was not there before

Mawiknat Sma'knis

O' Niskam ki'l mlkikno'tiktuk wejien
Sameka'tu npi'kunatkmn
Kulaman jiksitultes aq ma' siaw-tli-awnasita'siw
Nun'ji aq nsiskw sama'tu kulaman nmitutes ki'l kklu'sutim
Aq patkwietes.
Sameke'tu mikekne'l nutapsunn, naskmann wjit ni'n
teli-emteskin,
Tl-sama'tu nkutey nike' nipkewey wju'sn tel-wantaqe'k
Pasikn kutey wen pe'sklamijel
Kesalul O' Niskam mlkikno'tiktuk wejien.
Welsitm wju'sn ta'n tujiw stoqniktuk sapsik,
        kejitu wejuokw eimn.
Ta'n tujiw kiwaskikiskik nemitasik mlkiko'tim
Ki'l eimn te'sk wel-kisapniaq,
Wela'lin ta'n teli-iknmuin kina'matnewey,
ta'n asite'lmin siawi-klusin wjit ki'l.
Ki'limsit net pkwatuin
Mkisnmk tel-lapska'tasijik wjit ki'l
Ki'l siawa'sin wantaqo'timk,
Samtey elita'si siawi-tkweiwinen
Msit na wjit ki'l weliaqm
Kesalul Niskam aq iapjiw mui'walultes.

Prayer by Rita Joe
Translated as "The Great Brave"
by Murdena Marshall, March 27, 1990

We are the Dreamers

Correction Sheet

• The prayer on page 6 should read as follows:

Mawiknat Sma'knis

O' Niskam ki'l mlkikno'tiktuk wejien
Sameka'tu npi'kunatkm
Kulaman jiksitultes aq ma' siaw-tli-awnasita'siw
Nun'ji aq nsiskw sama'tu kulaman nmitutes ki'l kklu'sutim
Aq patkwietes.
Sameka'tu mikekne'l nutapsunn, naskmann wjit ni'n
Teli-emteskin,
Tl-sama'tu nkutey nike' nipkewey wju'sn tel-wantaqe'k
Pasik nkutey wen pe'sklamijel
Kesalul O' Niskam mlkikno'tiktuk wejien.
Welsitm wju'sn ta'n tujiw stoqniktuk sapsik,
     kejitu wejuow eimn.
Ta'n tujiw kiwa'skikiskik nemitasik mlkikno'tim
Ki'l eimn te's wel-kisapniaq,
Wela'lin ta'n teli-iknmuin kina'matnewey,
Ta'n teli-asite'lmin siawi-klusin wjit ki'l.
Ki'l, msit net pekwatuin
Mkisnmk tel-lapska'tasijik wjit ki'l
Ni'n siawa'sin wantaqo'timk,
Samte, elita'si siawi-tkweiwinen
Msit na wjit ki'l weliuqm
Kesalul Niskam aq iapjiw mui'walultes.

• Page 29:

Kmu'ji'japi' should read Kmu'ji'japi

Corrections continued on other side....

• <u>Page 36:</u>

Na' tujiw ntapekiaqnm na'ta'q <u>should read</u>
Na tujiw ntapekiaqnm na'ta'q

• <u>Page 49:</u>

Niskam-mijua'ji'j <u>should read</u> Niskam mijua'ji'j

• <u>Page 72:</u>

Malt elasnl Se'susal,
"Saqmaw, ula i'mu'sipn,
Mu pa npisoqq wijikitiekaq,
Skatu kejitu nike',
Kisu'lkw iknmultal msit ta'n tel-tamjl."

• <u>Page 76:</u>

L'nueyey iktuk <u>should read</u> L'nueyeyiktuk

While Dr. Bernie Francis generously served as our linguistic consultant on this project, these errors were made during the final proof reading in which he did not participate. We are grateful for the help Dr. Francis gave but it should be understood that responsibility for errors remains with the publisher.

Ronald Caplan,
Publisher,
Breton Books

The Great Brave

O' Niskam the Great Brave
Touch the feathers of my bonnet
So that my spirit may rise and not anxious as I was before
Lay your hand upon my brow
My shadow in tune to your goodness I bow.

Touch the leather I wear with humility
Touch it gently like a soft breeze
A gentle sigh.

I love you my Great Brave
I love the wind whisper through the trees.
The four seasons play and gone
The spiritual phenomena of early dawn.
The gift of knowledge so many ways
The woven eloquence you help me raise.
Touch my moccasins and the beads
That we may always represent you in peace
Touch them gently
They are the representation of my dreams.
I love you my Great Brave
I thank you.

I Salute the Sun

In the early morning warmth
I salute the sun.
You have brought me so much joy
My food my comfort.

As the noonday sun rolls across the sky
I give thanks to the One who made us.
Lifting my arms to the heavens
The simple greeting I share.

I do the same at its setting
Knowing the light and its meaning.
The knowledge known since the dawn of time
He comes as light, our humility shines.

Mikjikj (Turtle)

While I was in my kitchen in the basement
My two brothers came to visit,
 As they were going down the steps I heard Saln say
"Roddy, you are slow like a mikjikj"
 Immediately my native education needed a boost
"What is a mikjikj?"
 The two brothers spoke at the same time, "A turtle"
 I love you both, I said, though I never know why.
 A short while later on November 1980 Roddy disappeared
 Exactly two months later Saln died.

My kitchen has since been moved up
But every time I'm in the basement
 I visualize the two brothers walking in.
 With Roddy in the lead and Saln complaining:
"You are slow like a mikjikj,"
 And then I smile, because love is still there.

Saln — Charlie
mikjikj — turtle

9

Mattaqte'kn (A Message)

One early morning I recited the prayer to St. Therese
Re-read it again trying to translate into Mi'kmaw
Where it says a message of love I thought very hard
Mattaqte'kn I thought, the word of message in Mi'kmaw.
Ta'n teli-ksalimk (How I am loved)
The movement of prayer registering.
Where there was concern, gentleness
My mind settled and joy falling into place.
Just for uniting my thought on the word "message"
The image of the Little Flower cascaded like her roses.

Mattaqte'kn — a drumming, a message,
even a telegram or telephone
Mi'kmaw — Micmac

There is a Hill

In Eskasoni Reservation there is a hill
Where we the Micmac have put a cross.
It is there for us to realize
That we can climb as much as we want
The small hardship we may experience
Elita'suatmek ntalasutmaqnnen

In Eskasoni there is a hill I climb
It is steep and hard,
While climbing one day with my children
I thought I would never make it to the top
My thoughts turned to Simon of Cyrene
"Help me, Simon," I whispered
The climb was then easy on.

In Eskasoni there is a hill you may climb
There is a cross and the image of the Blessed Mother
You may climb as we do, especially on Good Friday
Then maybe we may look upon each other as friends
Like we want you to since the day you came.
Na ntalasutmaqnminal mawita'tal
Aq we'jitutesnu wlo'ti'.

Elita'suatmek ntalasutmaqnnen — We depend on our supplications
Na ntalasutmaqnminal mawita'tal — Our prayers will join
Aq we'jitutesnu wlo'ti' — We will find happiness.

There is much suffering after a vision

I had gone to a healer and the only way
I can say is the gears in motion of my heart and body.
The question on my part was, "Why heal one area?"
And not other. I was told, "He sees in your heart not you,"
I am glad He saw, the open door of my nkamlamun
I am glad He saw.
There is so much suffering after a vision.

Then there was a peace and the welcome sign
I had to go because it was where I was born.
The presence of a woman was felt, I voiced
The blue sun, the red sun, then the cloud
The fuzzy image of a woman, holding a baby.
When will it be clear? Will I see the woman again?
Is it my mother? She died with the baby inside her,
Or the Blessed One Who bore my Se'sus?
I do not know.
There was much suffering after the vision.

nkamlamun — my heart
Se'sus — Jesus

The Phone Call

At 1:30 am the phone rang in the other room
I rushed from the bedroom to answer.
A shadow appeared to block my path
I blurted out, "Frank, get out of my way"
I rushed through cold air.
I know I walked through the spirit of my husband
Amazement comes to mind as I write today.

I do not remember who was on the phone
Nor what was said.
The only part I remember is the cold air.

The spirit of our loved ones care
What goes on in their home.
Though they are not there
The concern is still there
The shadow roams.

Poor Man, Poor World

While I was writing my story
The telephone rang.
"I want to speak to Rita Joe."
"This is her speaking, Sir," I answered.
"Will you come to our school to speak?
I would appreciate it.
Whatever it is you speak about, basket weaving or what."
"I do not weave baskets, Sir.
I am a writer and speak about my culture."
"Whatever you do, speak to our children."
My phone went dead.
Poor man, poor world, I thought
The crooked world will never change.
I will though,
Putting a badge on my heart.
I will speak to his schoolchildren.
Maybe then, the next generation may not say
"Whatever it is you speak about, basket weaving or what."
Poor man, poor world.
I love his children, I am a determined Indian
I love his children and I have a heart.

The Kateri Tekewitha Conference in Orono, Maine, USA

On August 7, 1992, in Orono, Maine
My daughter Phyllis and I were at a conference.
The evening started with a healing service
To the thousands of people holding hands singing.
On either side I held hands, singing with my heart
I fell to the floor, the five senses there but paralysis set.
Finally I could get up, got in line to a healer. An Ojibwe
I saw him raise a hand to pray, fell again.
Later we went to a powwow, happy voices in song
And saw Mary Rose Julian give her mother turquoise prayer beads
Father Jim from Old Town Maine blessed them. The dance started
"Give me the beads," I told Sarah.
I held the beads close to my heart as I danced, thinking of Se'sus
An instant of eternity I had a vision, our beautiful Kattlin.
Tiredness followed, my bed a welcome sight at the University.
In the morning I heard weeping, and an incredible sight
Of flashing lights, like dancing small stars.
Gently I asked my daughter what she was dreaming
"Healing rings," she said. "Four large rings carried as if a banner."
The procession in the forest, the native environment in place.
"Let us go to the Sacred Fire Service," I said.
We attended the service, my mind in awe at what had transpired.
The people were from across the nation, Canada and USA
So very respectful of the good forces we do not see.
The name Tekewitha means She who stumbles and bumps into things.
In heaven she is doing the same, our beautiful Kattlin.

They Are There Just Behind the Wall

I awoke in pain
A feeling of great loneliness descended.
I am alone, my man is not with me
He has gone ahead, his promise ringing in my head,
"I will save a little space in heaven, not hog it all."
The memory hurt, I try to psyche it out.
My wish hanging in silence.
The loved ones just behind the wall
Yet I cannot reach them

My imploration is what keeps me going
The image brought on the mind.

Take care my children
I love you
Please love one another
No anger
Hug.

Weji-uli-Niskam (Holy Spirit)

O Holy Spirit whose eyes I see
If I ask.
His face I see on the cloud
The voice so gentle in a soft breeze.
The mantle of his cloak on the green.
The dust I would wash off his feet
If he asked.
O Holy Spirit please ask.
I am so small and weak
The broken body I hide
Behind the closed door.
Waiting for tomorrow and the next
Maybe the tremor will stop, just maybe.
I pray as I carry the cross, asking Simon to help.
O Holy Spirit I accept:
The joy is that I see
The joy is that I think
The joy is that I write
I acknowledge and salute my Niskam
I salute him again and again.
My tobacco is there, the sweetgrass ready,
The peace pipe is in my family.
O Holy Spirit I thank you.

My Shadow Follows

The drumsong fills the air
I dance as my heart fills with happiness.
My joy I give to others in spirit
Who need but are unable to express.
The ban still in place, put there long ago
Naming it pagan, they did not understand
My native word for God
Kisu'lkw (the One who made us)
I have had knowledge since the beginning.
That is why I looked to the sun
He shows himself as light
A beautiful light, no name only voice
We are part of the creation, the gentle
That is why I feel joy
My shadow follows, the revelation in place.

I know
As the drumsong fills the air
There was a reason for the writing.
My findings make me cry,
The tears sweet.
And the inspiration I do not leave,
Until I am no more but in the light.
This is the gift I am learning from.

Bradley Rose

He played with his toy, not really playing.
The bowed head, rattail and short.
Trying to find the reason
"Why isn't mommy here?"
There are no reasons, she is gone.
His child-mind does not know.
My heart was full of love I felt
My grandchild
But what can I do.

Only the hope to caress the body
And tell him I love him again and again.
That is all I can do, I am only the gramma
I too will be gone soon.
I love you kwi's, I love you
Over and all and even beyond.

kwi's — son

19

Wenmajita'si (I am filled with grief)

Kiskuk eksitpu'kek alasutmay
Etawey kisi wi'kiken
Etawey kisi ankita'sin
Etawey kijka' mlkikno'ti
Ma'w kitu'-kinua'tekey aq kekina'muey
We'jitutoqsip mu i'muann
Ankite'lmuloqop msit
Siaw-lukutikw nutqo'ltioq
Kisa'tutoqsip na.

Today, this morning I prayed
I ask to write a little longer
I ask if I may be able to think
I ask for a small strength
I still want to show, teach.
You will find when I am gone
I thought about all of you
Continue the work, you young people
You can do it.

Please Let Me Go

At 4 a.m. on December 1, I had awakened slightly ill
The illness I knew had to do with the heart.
To ease the pain was mostly on the mind
I put a rollaid in my mouth
And lay there waiting to ease the air.
There was no panic but pictures came to mind
A beautiful feeling that if I let go
I will see my Niskam, my Kisu'lkw, my Lord.
Finally I fell asleep, awakening later
To hear my children in the next room.

I just wanted to tell about the good feeling
When my time comes please let me go.

A Mi'kmaw Cure-all for Ingrown Toenail

I have a comical story for ingrown toenail
I want to share with everybody
The person I love and admire is a friend
This is her cure-all for an elderly problem
She bought rubber boots one size larger
And put salted water above the toe
Then wore the boots all day
When evening came the cut easy
The ingrown problem much better.
I laughed when I heard the story
It is because I have the same tender distress
So might try the Mi'kmaw cure-all
The boots are there, just add the salted water
And laugh away the pesky sore
I'm even thinking of bottling for later use.

Street Names

In Eskasoni, there were never any street names, just name areas.
There was Qam'sipuk (Across the river.)
74th Street now, you guess why the name.
Apamuek, central part of Eskasoni, the home of Apamu.
New York Corner, never knew the reason for the name.
There is Gabriel Street, the church Gabriel Centre.
Espíse'k, very deep water.
Beach Road, naturally the beach road.
Mickey's Lane. There must be a Mickey there.
Spencer's Lane, Spencer lives there, why not Arlene? His wife.
Cremo's Lane, the last name of many people.
Crane Cove Road, the location of Crane Cove Fisheries.
Pine Lane, a beautiful spot, like everywhere else in Eskasoni.
Silverwood Lane, the place of silverwood.
George Street, bet you can't guess who lives there.
Denny's Lane, the last name of many Dennys.
Paul's Lane, there are many Pauls, Poqqatla'naq.
Johnson Place, many Johnsons.
Morris Lane, guess who?
Horseshoe Drive, considering no horses in Eskasoni.
Beacon Hill, elegant place name,
I used to work at Beacon Hill Hospital in Boston.
Mountain Road,
A'nslm Road, my son-in-law Tom Sylliboy, daughter,
                three grandchildren live there
and Lisa Marie, their poodle.
Apamuekewawti, near where I live, come visit.

Someday They Will Listen

I am at the Writers and Publishers Conference
The theme is on Education.
I am a Mi'kmaw mingling with writers
My concern is the part we play in this century.
There is indifference, not fully understood
The traders still there
The discomfort on my part unsettled.
How do we bombard when only half listen?
The roar on the other side modern in its din.
I stand there listening to the many voices
The suppression adding to the loneliness.
Walking from one ballroom to the next
Realizing how small the existence is.
My nativeness fighting a lost war
A long time I think
My story inside of the heart unspoken
In the great ballroom of the elegant hotel.

The elders on my reservation said be patient
When all else is gone
They will listen.

Mi'kmaw Culture Is Like Looking Through a Window

My culture is like looking through a window
I see, hear, feel, smell, using the five senses
To do my bidding, researching my Indianness
And what I find makes it all the more interesting.
To know, to hear, to feel, to smell, to touch your heart
In my findings, the knowledge so beautiful
To behold.
It has been thirty-one years the year of 1998.
I find the Mi'kmaq so unusual that it floors me sometimes
But I keep going because they say I'm looking into my own soul
The eyes have a companion who steers,
        he is good, loving, my mentor.
I see sometimes the edge of wood, the trees waving their wares
I touch gently, not hurt,
        sensing the human-like quality of extra sense.
Oh yes, I am the Mi'kmaw walking through the forest like a king.
I see through the window what is there, it is beauty in raw
The make-shift wigwam when I was seven, my mattress
        the pine branches
I remember its comfort.
My older sister cooking at bonfire, the lu'sknikn tasting
        better than in the oven.
I remember the taste.
And hearing my dad speaking our language in kindness
        to scold or of love.
Oh yes, I am the Mi'kmaw walking like a king.

lu'sknikn — bread

25

A Heritage that Never Died

I hear my child speak an ancient language
Which is my own.
My native dress hangs in the closet
Waiting to be worn for a purpose.
A drawknife, a crooked knife are in my craft shop
I look at all these things together and say
They are still there, reality does not lie
I come from a heritage that never died.

At powwow grounds we dance the ko'jua
The drummers sing the old songs.
The sacred fire burns for many days
You pray the four directions.
The salutation to our Creator
Kisu'lkw is his name.
I come from a heritage that never died.

We are the same people old chronicles told
We were less than human, a story so cold.
I began my gentle war in my thirties
It is because of the coldness my children felt.
The feeling was passed to me as my knees trembled
Standing before countless audiences, a story told.
"A force was drawn," my heart daily cried
I come from a heritage that never died.

ko'jua — Mi'kmaq dance

Pqasaw

The best way to cook an eel
Is to grab the whole fish
Slide it around the wood ashes
Then wipe off the skmoqn
You do that several times until clean
Then wash, remove entrails
Cut the eel in half, lay flat
Be sure to cut into bone
You hang up to dry about 24 hours
Then cut into four to six inch
Laying each piece flat on bake pan
Cook about 45 minutes in 350 heat.
They will be cooked when they look crisp and brown
With bannock and strong tea, there is nothing better.

Pqasaw — flat eel
skmoqn — slime

Wetapeksi (My Ancestry)

Once my husband was writing up his family tree
I helped all I could, even doing mine.
There was a point where we could go no further
Because of no documents surviving time.
His ancestry went back to Ktaqmkuk and Potlotek
Mine to We'kopa'q and goodness knows where else.
The joke is on me, as far as he was concerned
The fun to the both of us I reasoned playfully
Ktaqmkuk and Potlotek had many boats landed
While We'kopa'q means the edge of water
They had nowhere else to go but be happy.

Ktaqmkuk — Newfoundland
Potlotek — Chapel Island
We'kopa'q — Whycocomagh

28

The Language the Empire of My Nation

I have such unique language, Se'sus for instance
Jesus in yours.
Wa'so'q
The heaven where you make it.
Wastew
Snow so beautiful as it falls in flakes.
Tupkwan
Mud or soil grows living things.
Stoqn
The balsam tree, its aroma no match.
Kmu'j
Wood we value more than its worth.
Kmu'ji'japi'
The maple tree, the emblem of Canada.
Alukji'j
The small cloud in the sky.
Musikisk
The blue sky.
Kloqoej
The star at night.
Ni'n
Me, I am a poet.
Ankita'si
I think what is right.
To teach you about my empire.
I have it all in my head.
Listen, the royalty may surprise you.

Newtnmi'k (One of a Kind)

Newtnmi'k L'nu'qamiksuti
Indianness is one of a kind.
Newtnmi'k telewo'kuti'kw
We speak in unique way.
Newtnmi'k kelu'lk ta'n we'jitu telo'lti'kw
I found one good way.
Aq mekite'tm
I think highly of it.

Coincidences
Pet-tla'sik (It Happens Accidentally)

My messages come in the most unlikely places
From people I do not know.
Unexpected,
Uncalled for,
They come.

I do not remember since when
Which one?
But they come.
How long?
I don't know.

Sometimes brushing by me
The blowing of wind on my face
When there is no wind.

Maybe it is because of cultivation in a garden
Where beauty grows
Together we nod
You listen, while I sow.

Grand Chief Gabriel Sylliboy 1873-1964

I was in St. Rita's Hospital on March 4, 1964
Dozing, when Mrs. Stephen Paul in the next room
Kept calling my name; I asked what is it?
She said our Grand Chief is very ill
He wants a Mi'kmaw to be with him.
I asked a nurse to take me in a wheelchair
So that I may honour his request.
He asked who I was. "I am the daughter of Josie Gould."
He pointed upward, "Josie is there. I will be with him soon."
I listened to his words, fascinated by his eloquence,
Meditating in my mind that he sees our Creator.
The nurse came to take me back to bed.
On my way I saw the elevator door open
Leonard Denny stepped out and headed for the room
Where I knew our Grand Chief was waiting.
"I am here to do anything you ask," Leonard told him
"A young lady was here a while ago. I wanted to ask her
Piskwasenmui kwi's wa'so'q (Son, light my way to heaven)"
Leonard thought quickly and produced a book of matches
Respecting the traditional plea of prayer.
To him the most honored Mi'kmaw was on his way home.
And he was glad to be there for him.
When Leonard and I shared our stories later, we both cried.
The Grand Chief of the Mi'kmaw Nation had done his work well
For forty-six years, he remained honourable
Today I salute him.

In Own Words

In Mi'kmaw I talk to Niskam
Not only on Sunday but other times.
I touch the earth whisper thank you
My thanksgiving for growing things.
In early morning I look to the sky
My vision is there, thank you
My mind is clear, thank you
The one finger typing, thank you.
In own words it is so easy
Like talking to somebody that is listening.
He helps those who help themselves.
I should know, my sickness is there
But he is my back-up.

The Man in Indian Jacket

In my bed one night I awaken to the sensation of touch
A man was peering down at me
As if with concern
A beautiful jacket hung on his lean frame
The fringes swinging with every move
His stride the sureness of man
The face I could not see it was circled in fog
Then he turned going through the wall
I jumped out of bed in search of him
And seeing the secure door, knew he was supernatural
I returned to my bed, placing a child on either side
Acting on what mother taught
The innocence of children
Reciting the Lord's Prayer,
My gaze holding the symbol on the wall
Soon I slept.
The next day I told my mother
"The in-laws," she said. "Ask them."
Sure enough, they had a relative
Who had a favourite jacket
The late Grand Chief John Denny
My in-law kin from another age.

Grand Chief John Denny died in 1919.

34

Blind But Clean

I was nine when I heard this story.

My sister Annabel in her teens and others
Were gathered at an area where young people go at night.
They heard a sound, like someone scrubbing the floor
They looked among the houses in the dark, until near one
There was a scrubbing sound inside. They knocked and went in
An old blind woman was kneeling and washing the floor.
One of the girls said, "Let us finish and tell us your story."
She said when young and able,
        she liked clean floors and everything
Now blind, she is still aware of anything not clean.
When babysitting she passed the time cleaning by touch.
The story stayed with me until now in my old age
The awareness is still in the mind, so young ones
Let us old folks do what little we can
Being needed is what keeps our hearts going, we do small
But satisfaction puts everything in perspective.

Ntapekiaqnm na na'ta'q
(My Song Is Fading)

My song is fading, I realize
As I try to write, I cry.
But then again I think of the blessings
My gentle war of words have brought.
They touched all nations
The more in sorrow than anger
Na' tujiw ntapekiaqnm na'ta'q
And on this land I stand I am a stranger.

You can change that part
Sing along with me

Na' tujiw ntapekiaqnm na'ta'q — That is when my song fades

There Is Life Everywhere

The ever-moving leaves of a poplar tree lessened my anxiety as I walked through the woods trying to make my mind work on a particular task I was worried about. The ever-moving leaves I touched with care, all the while talking to the tree. "Help me," I said. There is no help from anywhere, the moving story I want to share. There is a belief that all trees, rocks, anything that grows is alive, helps us in a way that no man can ever perceive, let alone even imagine. I am a Mi'kmaw woman who has lived a long time and know which is true and not true, you only try if you do not believe, I did, that is why my belief is so convincing to myself. There was a time when I was a little girl, my mother and father had both died and living at yet another foster home which was far away from a native community. The nearest neighbours were non-native and their children never went near our house, though I went to their school and got along with everybody, they still did not go near our home. It was at this time I was so lonely and wanted to play with other children my age which was twelve at the time. I began to experience unusual happiness when I lay on the ground near a brook just a few meters from our yard. At first I lay listening to the water, it seemed to be speaking to me with a comforting tone, a lullaby at times. Finally I moved my playhouse near it to be sure I never missed the comfort from it. Then I developed a friendship with a tree near the brook, the tree was just there, I touched the outside bark, the leaves I did not tear but caressed. A comforting feeling spread over me like warmth, a feeling you cannot experience unless you believe, that belief came when I was sad-dest. The sadness did not return after I knew that comfort-able unity I shared with all living animals, birds, even the well I drew the water from. I talked to every bird I saw, the trees received the most hugs. Even today I am sixty-six years old, they do not know the unconditional freedom I have experienced from the knowledge of knowing that this is possible. Try it and see. There is life everywhere, treat it as it is, it will not let you down.

A Sea of Flowers

In the predawn time of morning I awaken
I see a sea of flowers in every color
There were roses, carnations, tulips and others
And splashes of green at intervals like leaves.
This only happened with closed eyes, when open nothing
I tested the phenomena over and over again.
Pinching myself, slapping my face
Amazement beyond any knowledge before this happened.
So I sat up and wondered if this was part of my illness
My mind then settled.
Alasutmay
If it is part of my illness, it is beautiful

Alasutmay — I pray

Ankita'si (I think)

A thought is to catch an idea
Between two minds.
Swinging to and fro
From English to Native,
Which one will I create, fulfill
Which one to roll along until arriving
To settle, still.

I know, my mind says to me
I know, try Mi'kmaw...
Ankite'tm
Na kelu'lk we'jitu (I find beauty)
Ankite'tm
Me' we'jitutes (I will find more)
Ankita'si me' (I think some more).

We'jitu na!

We'jitu na — I find!

Plawej and L'nui'site'w
(Partridge and Indian-Speaking Priest)

Once there was an Indian-speaking priest
Who learned Mi'kmaw from his flock.
He spoke the language the best he knew how
But sometimes got stuck.
They called him L'nui'site'w out of respect to him
And loving the man, he meant a lot to them.
At specific times he heard their confessions
They followed the rules, walking to the little church.
A widow woman was strolling through the village
On her way there, when one hunter gave her a day-old plawej
She took the partridge, putting it inside her coat
Thanking the couple, going her way.
At confession, the priest asked, "What is the smell?"
In Mi'kmaw she said, "My plawej."
He gave blessing and sent her on her way.
The next day he gave a long sermon, ending with the words
"Keep up the good lives you are leading,
                    but wash your plawejk."
The women giggled, he never knew why.
To this day there is a saying, they laugh and cry.
Whatever you do, wherever you go
Always wash your plawejk.

I Washed His Feet

In early morning she burst into my kitchen. "I got something to tell you, I was disrespectful to him," she said. "Who were you disrespectful to?" I asked. "Se'sus," she said. I was overwhelmed by her statement. Caroline is my second youngest. How in the world can one be disrespectful to someone we never see? It was in a dream, there were three knocks on the door. I opened the door, "Oh my God you're here." He came in but stood against the wall. "I do not want to track dirt on your floor," he said. I told him not to mind the floor but come in, that tea and lu'sknikn will be ready in a moment. He ate and thanked me.... But then he asked if I would wash his feet, he looked kind and normal, but a bit tired. In the dream, she said, I took an old t-shirt and wet it with warm water and washed his feet, carefully cleaning them, especially between his toes. I wiped them off and put his sandals back on. After I was finished I put the TV on, he leaned forward looking at the television. His hair fell forward, he pushed it away from his face. I removed a tendril away from his eye. "I am tired of my hair," he said. "Why don't you wear a ponytail or have it braided?" He said all right but asked me to teach him how to braid. I stood beside him and touched his soft hair and saw a tear in his eye, using my pinky finger to wipe the tear away. He smiled gently. I then showed him how to braid his hair, guiding his hands on how it was done. He caught on real easy. He was happy. He thanked me for everything. You are welcome any time you want to visit. He smiled as he walked out. He is just showing us he is around at any time, even in 1997. I was honoured to hear the story firsthand.

lu'sknikn — bannock

42

Apiksiktuaqn
(To forgive, be forgiven)

A friend of mine in Eskasoni Reservation
Entered the woods and fasted for eight days.
I awaited the eight days to see him
I wanted to know what he learned from the sune'wit
To my mind this is the ultimate for a cause
Learning the ways, an open door, derive.
At the time he did it, it was for
                    the people, the oncoming powwow
The journey to know, rationalize, spiritual growth.
When he came home I asked to see him
When he drew near, a feeling like a parent on me
He was my son, I wanted to listen.
He talked fast, at times with a rush of words
As if to relate all, but sadness took over.
I hugged him and said, "Don't talk if it is too sad."
The spell was broken, he could say no more.
The one thing I heard him say, "Apiksiktuaqn nuta'ykw"
For months it stayed on my mind.
Now it may go away as I write
Because this is the past, the present, the future.

I wish this would happen to all of us
Unity then will be the world over
My friend carried a message
Let us listen.

> sune'wit — to fast, abstain from food
>
> Apiksiktuaqn nuta'ykw — To forgive, be forgiven

43

Command of Language

I know some ladies on my reservation
They married for love and communication
They are not native in skin and tone
But you would think so by hearing their word.
They learned to speak Mi'kmaw by determination
Their children fluent by imitation.
The command is there if you are sure
The language of your loved ones so dear.

A Sad Comedy

At 12:30 a.m. I was reading
When I got sleepy.
And in order to still my trembling arm
I have to lay on the left side, to stop the tremor,
I was on the right side so tried to turn
To position the body to the left for comfort.
As I turned I hit my nose, blood flowed
I tried not to get any on the carpet
To the bathroom my body stumbled
The nose bled for five minutes
I trembled from the cold, hoping that it stop
Cleaned the sink, so others not see the mess.
I stuck a piece of tissue up my nose
Hoping not to bleed to the end.
Sleep came quickly, waking two hours later
The tissue was removed, gave thanks
A sad comedy on my part, no one knew
Only a memory and a giggle to myself.

In Order of Line

In my country
I am like a left-handed compliment.
Still the round-shouldered native
Stumbling over his mukluks.
Or maybe the wise pariah to hold at arm's length
With no say.

In my country
At least I am second in line
In order of mounties, natives and snow.
But still with no say.
But on my Indian Reservation we are slow to anger
For five hundred years we bit our tongue
Until now
I want my country to know
Natives are No. 1, then mounties, then finally the snow.

A Guide

One time my suffering was so great
I thought I was losing my mind.
The thought in my head was to get help
In the only way I knew how.
Get out of the house, no matter what
Publicize the problem, ask others for help.
This is what I did, and inside the institution
He still came, claiming the title of ownership.
I told my physician, why couldn't I be protected.
Arrangements were made, somehow not kept.
Finally I became desperate, relying on spiritual help.
Sure enough, I received a warning when trouble was near.
Something brushing near me, something so near
I could smell the tanned leather, my dad use to wear.
Our loved ones help us when we are down
Their aura only felt, the soul spiritual bound.
But they help us, now I know
Because sometime when I am down I think of my dad
He is not here anymore but the sound of his footfall
My strength returns like a butterfly
I lift away the hurt inside, secretly I smile.

We are the Dreamers

In the dream I saw my dad come in
He was carrying a vacuum cleaner
I have brought a present he said
This is nothing strange, he has been dead a few years.
I told my mother about it, "Something good will happen."
The next day, she received a lot of money.
The people in our community call us the dreamers
I do not mind it one bit.
I like the part about beautiful dreams
My dad comes in many of them, my daughter, too
She is the Native Angel my mom speaks about
They usually come to solve a problem, show good
The most of our kin who loved us in life, still do
They communicate the love in so many ways
My dad's laughter shows the good side
And bringing of the present a message
My mother knows, we separate when one is gone
But the caring power remains, the love living on
We should know, we are the dreamers
To the most of us, it is a bond.

The Manger

I thought of Christmas with garlands and tree
I thought of presents to wrap and name.
The cooking to be done, to clean
Then weariness took over, an idea came.
Trivial expectations the thoughts are
Why not a manger, thinking to myself.
This is what this time is all about
Niskam-mijua'ji'j, whose birthday it is.

A bell rang in my aged mind
A sketch on plywood, a Holy Family.
With a cow, a donkey, even a lamb
A shelter of hay in Bethlehem.
With a spotlight shining to the image
My production brought good feeling.

Now people pass by with a lingering gaze
They look at my humble Bethlehem.
The manger is there enjoyed by all
My masterpiece a perfection down to the stall.
This is what Christmas is all about
A happy birthday to Niskam-mijua'ji'j

Niskam-mijua'ji'j — God-baby

49

Mother Earth's Hair

On August 1989 my husband and I were in Maine
Where he died, I went home alone in pain.
We had visited each reservation we knew
Making many friends, today I still know.
Near a road a woman was sitting on the ground
She was carefully picking strands of grass
Discarding some, holding others straight
I asked why was she picking so much.
She said, "They are ten dollars a pound."
My husband and I sat alongside of her, becoming friends
A bundle my husband picked then, later my treasure.
I know, as all L'nu'k know,

      that sweetgrass is mother earth's hair
So dear in my mind my husband picking shyly for me
Which he never did before, in two days he will leave me.
Today as in all days I smell sweetgrass, I think of him
Sitting there so shy, the picture remains dear.

L'nu — aboriginal person

The Trembling Hand

My hand trembles as if some force is shaking it
It is Parkinson's, they say.
Thoughts enter my mind
"We're here!"
Who, I ask
The hand trembles again
Accept, don't ask
My spirit is down, whoever you are
I am my own boss.

Weji-uli-Niskam, apoqnmui
The hand stops trembling.

Weji-uli-Niskam — Holy Spirit

We Teach

Me' tali-wlo'ltioq?
How are you?

Ta'n kekinua'tekey nike'
What I am showing today

Kelu'lk wjit na kikmanaq.
It is good for our people.

Weli-kina'mua'ti'kw amuj pa
We have to teach well

Kulaman naji wli-nenuksitesnu
So others may know more about us

Aq kekinua'taqatiek ta'n teliaq kiskuk
We show what is happening today

Listukuj   Sweat

On June 21st, 1993 in Listukuj, Quebec
I entered a sweatlodge with twelve women
The conductor of the sweat was a Penobscot from Maine
A woman and her knowledge I relied upon as true
Because my sincerity in heart was going to be acted upon
To seek answers from all that is good about my culture
I entered the lodge on my knees instantly asking for my ancestors
My Creator to help me to understand the spiritual forces
The learning I knew we must all know before we receive answers.
The red-hot stones glowed in the dark receiving the water
The sweat rolling down the body cleaning as well as the mind
Expectation gradually awakening the senses the most in need
We act upon as we prod the unknown to follow up.
Lo and behold it is happening what I wish to be
The touching felt like feathers soft and soothing to the body
My broken speech unlike my own as I listened to the message.
The blue rays of light I tried to see better lifting my arms
I never wanted to let them go as they communicated the beauty
But at last saying the words "Wela'lioq pejitaioq apajita'q Wa'so'q."
The spell broken as the conductor said the words, "Open the door."
I was the second last to leave the lodge, then the Penobscot woman
The glow of the bonfire a welcome sight as I gave the doorman a hug
Then raising my eyes to the sky thanking my Creator, "Wela'lin."
The five-hour sweat was worth it, the communication was instant
All I can say is, "Niskam wela'lin, wela'lin."

When I am gone

The leaves of the tree will shiver
Because aspen was a friend one time.
Black spruce, her arms will lay low
And across the sky the eagle fly.
The mountains be still
Their wares one time like painted pyramids.
All gold, orange, red splash like we use on face.
The trees do their dances for show
Like once when she spoke
I love you all.
Her moccasin trod so softly, touching mother
The rocks had auras after her sweat
The grass so clean, she pressed it to cheek
Every blade so clean like He wants you to see.
The purification complete.
"Kisu'lkw" you are so good to me.
I leave a memory of laughing stars
Spread across the sky at night.
Try counting, no end, that's me, no end.
Just look at the leaves of any tree, they shiver
That was my friend, now yours
Poetry is my tool, I write.

End

We are the
Dreamers

BOOK TWO

Poems of Rita Joe

POEMS TO 1978

1

I am the Indian,
And the burden
Lies yet with me

2

My words fall,
Arousing inquisitiveness,
Hoping to stir
Different opinions.

If Indians today
Are not fictitious,
Then know them.

I am not
What they portray me.
I am civilized.
I am trying
To fit in this century.

Pray,
Meet me halfway—
I am today's Indian.

3

Before the white man came, we had our own political,
educational and economic way of life which followed the
teachings of our elders. But with restrictions on hunting, the
traditional native education is suppressed.

I lament forgotten skills,
While my deeds come from a new image.
Companion wind bewails over the hills
The fall from our customs and heritage.

Regret stays with me.
I reflect upon myself, unforgiving;
Uncertainty returns to haunt
The native ways I abandoned.

The years barely leave a trace
But the sun's warmth reminds my senses
Not to yield completely.

4

Your buildings, tall, alien,
Cover the land;
Unfeeling concrete smothers,
        windows glint
Like water to the sun.
No breezes blow
Through standing trees;
No scent of pine lightens my burden.

I see your buildings rising skyward,
        majestic,
Over the trails where once men walked,
Significant rulers of this land
Who still hold the aboriginal title
In their hearts
By traditions known
Through eons of time.

Relearning our culture is not difficult,
Because those trails I remember
And their meaning I understand.

While skyscrapers hide the heavens,
They can fall

5

Need you think
That I am unaware
Of others' cold stares—
The small attempts of communication.
Do you ever wonder
Why I am afraid to approach you,
To express my love
Of my tradition?

Need you wonder why
I do not kiwa'ska'siw
To your convictions.
All opinions are
Too deeply rooted
For only one solution.
Try
To accept beliefs as I,
As this is all we own.

6

Wen net ki'l?
Pipanimit nuji-kina'muet ta'n jipalk.
Netakei, aq i'-naqawey;
Koqoey?

Ktikik nuji-kina'masultite'wk kimelmultijik.
Na epa'si, taqawajitutm,
Aq elui'tmasi
Na na'kwek.

Espi-kjijiteketes,
Ma' jipajita'siw.
Espitutmikewey kina'matneweyiktuk eyk,
Aq kinua'tuates pa' qlaiwaqnn ni'n nikmaq.

                    Who are you?
                    Question from a teacher feared.
                    Blushing, I stammered
                    What?

                    Other students tittered.
                    I sat down forlorn, dejected,
                    And made a vow
                    That day

                    To be great in all learnings,
                    No more uncertain.
                    My pride lives in my education,
                    And I will relate wonders to my people.

7

Like lava from the heart
This wonder grows,
Why was a tale not told?
Admiration I know for the deeds
        of my people —
Their perceptions.

I know their wants
I know their ways
I know their creeds.

Their love of customs
Observance of rules.

Aknutm te' sɨk kejitu.

8

The acted role of an Indian,
A character assumed wrong.
The continuous misinterpretations
Of a life
That is hurting.

Echoes climb,
Distorted
Endlessly by repeated lies.
An undertow of current time.

Will it ever die?
Loosen the bond.
Undo?
Will not this relating ease

So that we may rest,
Performance over
And unravel the mistake—
Stories told
Of Indians and white men.

9

I

They say that I must live
A white man's way.
This day and age
Still being bent to what they say,
My heart remains
Turned to native time.

I must dress conservative in style
And have factory shoes upon my feet.
Leave the ways they say
Are wild.
Forfeit a heritage
That is conquered.

I must accept what this century
Has destroyed and left behind—
The innocence of my ancestry.

I must forget father sky
And mother earth,
And hurt this land we love
With towering concrete.

II

If I must fight
Their war as well,
Or share in conquests
And slip away in drink or drugs,
All wished for wealth
Is mockery to me.

My body yields, wanting luxuries,
But my heart reverts
To so-called savagery.

If we are slow
Embracing today's thoughts,
Be patient with us a while.
Seeing
What wrongs have been wrought,
Native ways seem not so wild.

10

Ai! Mu knu'kwaqnn,
Mu nuji-wi'kikaqnn,
Mu weskitaqawikasinukul kisna
    mikekni-napuikasinukul
Kekinua'tuenukul wlakue'l
    pa'qalaiwaqnn.

Ta'n teluji-mtua'lukwi'tij nuji-
    kina'mua'tijik a.

Ke' kwilmi'tij,
Maqamikewe'l wisunn,
Apaqte'l wisunn,
Sipu'l;
Mukk kasa'tu mikuite'tmaqnmk
Ula knu'kwaqnn.

Ki' welaptmikl
Kmtne'l samqwann nisitk,
Kesikawitkl sipu'l.
Ula na kis-napui'kmu'kl
Mikuite'tmaqanminaq.
Nuji-kina'masultioq,
    we'jitutoqsip ta'n kisite'tmekl
Wisunn aq ta'n pa'qi-klu'lk,
Tepqatmi'tij L'nu weja'tekemk
    weji-nsituita'timk.

10 (in English)

Aye! no monuments,
No literature,
No scrolls or canvas-drawn pictures
Relate the wonders of our yesterday.

How frustrated the searchings
        of the educators.

Let them find
Land names,
Titles of seas,
Rivers;
Wipe them not from memory.
These are our monuments.

Breathtaking views—
Waterfalls on a mountain,
Fast flowing rivers.
These are our sketches
Committed to our memory.
Scholars, you will find our art
In names and scenery,
Betrothed to the Indian
        since time began.

11

To the Indian
Peace is not a place
Where you stop
And worry no longer.

To the Indian
Peace is the ease of mind
Of being able to worry
Without being afraid.

12

Images from the past—
Of the man in the bush.
Wekayi in mind
To alter the picture.

You see me as I am,
A conquered master of this land;
I see myself the same,
But still I fight.

Otium cum dignitate.
So shall we,
A people least thought of,
Attain grace.

13

There is a tale of the men of peace,
The quiet ones.
The wise elders
And modern sons.

L'nu
Left no records,
But his beliefs continue,
And his ceremonial dress remains.

The lore and legends
Are not to be lost.
To say they are vanishing is
Not true.

In accepting new ways
Native life has changed.
Yet, reattracted to the traditions,
They are practiced again.

These are still the men of tomorrow.
The proud races,
The men of peace,
The quiet ones.

14

Kiknu na ula maqmikew
Ta'n asoqmisk wju'sn kmtnji'jl
Aq wastewik maqmikew
Aq tekik wju'sn.

Kesatm na telite'tm L'nueymk,
Paqlite'tm, mu kelninukw koqoey;
Aq ankamkik kloqoejk
Wejkwakitmui'tij klusuaqn.
Nemitaq ekel na tepknuset tekik wsiskw
Elapekismatl wta'piml samqwan-iktuk.

Teli-ankamkuk
Nkutey nike' kinu tepknuset
Wej-wskwijinuulti'kw,
Pawikuti'kw,
Tujiw keska'ykw, tujiw apaji-ne'ita'ykw
Kutey nike' mu pessipketenukek
        iapjiweyey.

Mimajuaqnminu siawiaq
Mi'soqo kikisu'a'ti'kw aq nestuo'lti'kw.
Na nuku' kaqiaq.
Mu na nuku'eimukkw,
Pasik naqtmu'k
L'nu' qamiksuti ta'n mu nepknukw.

14 (In English)

Our home is this country
Across the windswept hills
With snow on fields.
The cold air.

I like to think of our native life,
Curious, free;
And look at the stars
Sending icy messages.
My eyes see the cold face of the moon
Cast his net over the bay.

It seems
We are like the moon—
Born,
Grow slowly,
Then fade away, to reappear again
In a never-ending cycle.

Our lives go on
Until we are old and wise.
Then end.
We are no more,
Except we leave
A heritage that never dies.

15

The customs of various tribes
Are many.
The Mi'kmaw observe the rules
Of guiding traditions.

When a native dies, immediate supplications for the dead are said by a member of the family or the nearest relative. Then they wait with the prepared body for a three day wake, at which native prayers and hymns are sung and food and comfort given freely.

Then the Mass for the dead is sung by the priest and we answer prayers by the priest in Micmac. The hymns that we hear in our own tongue often move the native people to tears, for they are more beautiful to us heard in our own language.

When the body is being lowered into the ground, the native choir members sing a hymn that has been handed down for centuries:

Malt elasnl Se'susl,
Saqmaw, ula i'mu'sipn,
Mu pa npɨsoqq wijikitiekaq,
Skatu kejitu nike',
Kisu'lkw iknmultal msit ta'n tel-tamjl.

Then the Grand Chief tells the people that there will be a

gathering at the community hall where food, donated by the
people from the reservation, is served to the other
visitors. Then the deceased's personal belongings and dona-
tions from the people are gathered together and an auction
is held. There are instances where people will give the last
they have to the auction. Then, when it is over, the bills are
paid and if any money is left, it goes to the surviving family.

Habits of old
Our elders teach;
We honour, and we tell.

16

At age seven
To Springhill Jct. we came,
My father and I
And sister Annabel.

There we made our home
Of birchbark and pole
And a bed of pine branches.
I remember its comfort.

This was my home
A memory stands out—
A wigwam on the hill
In nineteen thirty-eight.

17

When I was small
I used to help my father
Make axe handles.
Coming home from the wood with a bundle
Of maskwi, snawey, aqmoq,
My father would chip away,
Carving with a crooked knife,
Until a well-made handle appeared,
Ready to be sand-papered
By my brother.

When it was finished
We started another,
Sometimes working through the night
With me holding a lighted shaving
To light their way
When our kerosene lamp ran dry.

Then in the morning
My mother would be happy
That there would be food today
When my father sold our work.

18

At early dawn of man
The Micmac invented ways
Of storing, to continue life.

One staple
Was moose butter—
After the meat is removed
The bones of the moose are collected,
Pounded with rocks
Reduced to powder,
Then placed in a kettle
And boiled well,
Bringing the grease atop
Which is collected
With a wooden spoon.
Without counting the marrow
Much grease is obtained.
Cooled
It becomes white as snow,
Firm as wax.

Good nourishment,
This they called qamu—
Moose butter.

19

Klusuaqnn mu nuku' nuta'nukul
Tetpaqi-nsɨtasin.
Mimkwatasik koqoey wettaqne'wasik
　　　L'nueyey iktuk ta'n keska'q
Mu a'tukwaqn eytnukw klusuaqney
　　　panaknutk pewatmɨkewey
Ta'n teli-kjijituekɨp seyeimɨk

Espe'k L'nu'qamiksuti,
Kelo'tmuinamɨtt ajipjɨtasuti.
Apoqnmui kwilm nsɨtuowey
Ewikasik ntinink,
Apoqnmui kaqma'si;
Pitoqsi aq melkiknay.

Mi'kmaw na ni'n;
Mukk skmatmu piluey koqoey wja'tuin.

19 (In English)

Words no longer need
Clear meanings.
Hidden things proceed from a lost legacy.
No tale in words bares our desire, hunger,
The freedom we have known.

A heritage of honour
Sustains our hopes.
Help me search the meaning
Written in my life,
Help me stand again
Tall and mighty.

Mi'kmaw I am;
Expect nothing else from me.

20

She spoke of paradise
And angels' guests.
She spoke of Niskam
and the Holy Spirit.
She spoke religiously
Of man's true brotherhood.
Yet once when she must sit beside me,
She stood.

21

A thousand ages we see
In a space of a moment,
And burdens follow
Out of old chronicles.

Submission I say, to obtain harmony,
But let the words die, that were written

So my children may see
The glories of their forefathers,
And share the pride of history

That they may learn
The way of their ancestors,
And nourish a quiet way.

Our children read and hate
The books offered—
A written record of events
By the white men.

Compromise I say, and meet
        our requirement,
Place the learning seed of happiness
        between us.

22

I have served prison terms
With locks on the door
For others' useless crimes.
My crime was being poor.
I'm in prison now,
Of freedom have I none

And the cry of this lonely heart—
I'll do no wrong again.

I did not understand
The reason or the need
To lock the prison door.
When seeing who I was
My pleading was in vain—
I cannot go.

An Indian in a cell—
A life he does not know.

My beliefs I have not told
To any living soul,
Being locked away
Behind the prison bars,
A passion for my freedom
Is my only goal.

I was free before
In spaces to the stars.

23

We make baskets of ash and maple.
Good wood.
Intricate designs, carefully woven,
     nothing crude,
Perfection binding.

Women of peace,
We weave each day.

24

I lay my body upon the ground
Feel each blade of grass—
Feel one with the earth.
This is my satisfaction.
I see the stars twinkling, and
Wish myself free of unwanted stumblings;
The wrongs undo and hurts dissolve.

My body lies upon the grass.
Peaceful odours of the wood
And dreams of my people filter past—
Images of when I was a child,
My father, my mother,
A smile present.

My body lay on the earth floor.
Reality came when I awoke,
Breaking the images of ages before.
In a lost fantasy
Desires broke without reason.

Kejitu mu telianukw
Katu wel'te'tm

25

They made their dishes of bark, sewn with fir roots so well
they held water.
They gathered dry fuel which did not smoke in the wigwam.
Their kettles made of wood always had soup to feed
family and stranger.
They hunted fur-bearing animals, dressed skins,
made clothing and moccasins, corded snowshoes, put
up and took down wigwams.
These and many other things kept the L'nu working

26

There is a hill, a watching place
Where we see the rivers entering Bras d'Or
That is where we float on still waters
Rafts made of spruce
With suspended scalloped shells
Waiting for spatfall.

With expectation we wait
For the spark of life to cling,
In the warm waters of Bras d'Or,
To the shells hanging by wire
On pontoons of spruce.
We wait for spatfall.

There is a hill, a watching place
From where we see our labours
Scattered on the waters
With bobbing buoys, a marking place
Of pontoons of spruce
We wait for spatfall.

We are the Mi'kmaw
As old as the sea.
With expectation of advancement
We foster nature,
Farming oysters
Around the fiords, near where we live.

Glossary

Aknutm	I'm telling...
Aqmoq	white ash
Katu	but
Kejitu	I know
Kiwa'ska'siw	(I do not) change, turn around
L'nu	native person
Maskwi	birchbark
Mi'kmaw	Micmac
Mu telianukw	not true
Niskam	God
Snawey	rock maple
Te'sɨk	that much
Wekayi	(I am) angry
Wel'te'tm	(I am) pleased about it

Malt elasnl Se'susl	Martha said to Jesus
Saqmaw, ula i'mu'sɨpn	Lord, if you had been here
Mu pa npɨsoqq wijikɨtiekaq	My brother would not have died
Skatu kejitu nike'	But I know that even now
Kisu'lkw iknmultal msɨt ta'n	God will give you whatever you
tel-tamjl	ask of him

Rita Joe

Born in Whycocomagh, Cape Breton Island, Rita Joe lives and writes and operates her craft shop in Eskasoni. She is the recipient of several awards including the Order of Canada and an Honorary Doctor of Laws from Dalhousie University. Her books include **Poems of Rita Joe** (Abanaki Press), **L'nu and Indians We're Called** and **Song of Eskasoni: More Poems by Rita Joe**, and **Song of Rita Joe: Autobiography of a Mi'kmaq Poet** (Ragweed). With Leslie Choyce, she edited **The Mi'kmaq Anthology** (Pottersfield Press).

I was only a housewife with a dream
To bring laughter to the sad eyes of my people,
And trusting the anchor we live by
To complete the woven tale we are still telling.

CAPE BRETON QUARRY
by STEWART DONOVAN

A book of poetry that gravitates between rural and urban Cape Breton Island, and the experience of working away. Stewart Donovan has written a relaxed, accessible set of poems of a man's growing up and his reflections on the near and distant past of his communities. A lovely, lasting little book.

$11.00

STORIES FROM
THE WOMAN FROM AWAY
by TESSIE GILLIS

"It's a very frightening book"—and one of the finest novels Cape Breton ever produced. Presenting a woman's life, and the men and women whose struggles, weaknesses and wit enrich her rural community, it delivers with unparalleled intensity a bold, rare portrait of the Maritimes.

$18.50

JOHN R. AND SON
and Other Stories
by TESSIE GILLIS

No one has ever written about Cape Breton quite like this. A rich, daring short novel, plus 5 stories, this troubling, brutal, compassionate book is a riveting minor classic.

$18.50

THE DAY THE MEN
WENT TO TOWN
16 Stories by Women from Cape Breton

Strong writing by women who have a significant attachment to Cape Breton Island! These stories are about fisherwomen and aliens from space, the poignancy of family life and tragedy in the coal mines. They are about several approaches to love. By Claudia Gahlinger, Lynn Coady, Joan Clark, Beatrice MacNeil, Susan Zettell, Sherry D. Ramsey, Jean McNeil, Kim Williamson, Tessie Gillis, Ann-Marie MacDonald, D.C. Troicuk, Tricia Fish, Erin McNamara, Teresa O'Brien, Ellen Frith, Carol Bruneau.

$18.50

WILD HONEY
by AARON SCHNEIDER

Stark and sensual, even sexy—funny and frightening by turns—these are poems you can read and read again, for enjoyment and for insight. By an award-winning writer, a teacher and an environmentalist who has made his life in Cape Breton.

$13.00

GOD & ME
by SHEILA GREEN

A gentle way of sharing wonder and relationship with a child, and a lovely keepsake for any adult: 18 open, unpretentious poems; 7 drawings by Alison R. Grapes.

$9.00

THE IRISH IN CAPE BRETON
by A. A. MacKENZIE

The best general introduction to the Irish experience and their contribution to Cape Breton Island. Rich with details of culture and individuals. With Paul M. MacDonald's essay "Irish Music in Cape Breton."

$16.25

THE HIGHLAND HEART
IN NOVA SCOTIA
by NEIL MacNEIL

Told with the pride and joy that only an exiled son can bring to the world of his heart and his childhood—wonderful writing about the peace and raw humour of Celtic Cape Breton's Golden Age. Raised at the turn of the century, Neil MacNeil became an editor of *The New York Times*.

$18.50

CASTAWAY ON CAPE BRETON
Two Great Shipwreck Narratives

1. Ensign Prenties' *Narrative* of Shipwreck at Margaree Harbour, 1780 (Edited with an Historical Setting and Notes by G. G. Campbell)
2. Samuel Burrows' *Narrative* of Shipwreck on the Cheticamp Coast, 1823 (With Notes on Acadians Who Cared for the Survivors by Charles D. Roach)

$13.00

• PRICES INCLUDE GST & POSTAGE IN CANADA •

CONTINUED ON NEXT PAGE